Reasoning

AGE 9-11

Alastair Pollitt

As a parent, you can play a major role in your child's education by your interest and encouragement. This book is designed to help improve your child's performance in the kinds of test commonly used for school selection and entrance examinations. By practising the various types of reasoning exercise at home, your child will become more confident in tackling them under examination conditions.

It is divided into five sections, each dealing with a particular kind of reasoning:

A   Picture Reasoning
B   Verbal Reasoning: Problems
C   Verbal Reasoning: Symbols
D   Verbal Reasoning: Concepts
E   Non-verbal Reasoning

Answers to all the questions are given at the back of the book.

Hodder Children's Books

NCPTA

The only home learning programme supported by the NCPTA

How to help your child

● Explain calmly to your child what has to be done in each section and make sure he or she understands how to record the answers.

● This book can be used purely for practice. However, if you wish to use it to simulate test conditions, you should set time limits as follows: 25 minutes for Section A, 40 minutes each for Sections B to D, and 30 minutes for Section E.

● If your child gets answers wrong, talk through the questions and try to find out if a particular type of question causes more problems than others. If so, concentrate on practising this type.

● Make sure that both you and your child approach this book as an enjoyable challenge, rather than an unpleasant chore. Concentrate on your child's successes and give plenty of praise and encouragement.

Published by Hodder Children's Books 1995

10 9 8 7

ISBN 0 340 65113 X

Copyright © Hodder Children's Books

Printed and bound in Great Britain

Hodder Children's Books
A division of Hodder Headline plc
338 Euston Road
London NW1 3BH

Previously published as Test Your Child's Reasoning Ability

A. Picture Reasoning

Draw a line through the picture which doesn't belong to the set.

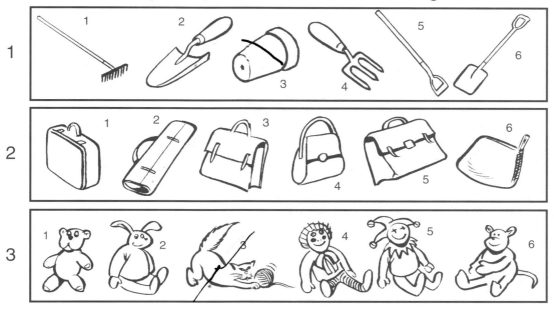

Draw a line through the picture which has something wrong with it.

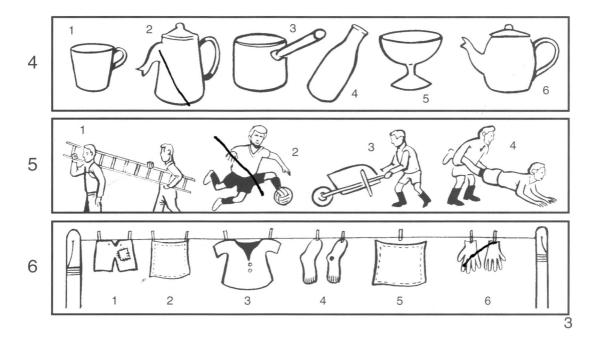

↓ is to ↓ as ↓ is to .....Draw a line through *one* picture.

Draw a line through the picture which has something wrong with it.

Sort these pictures into the best order. Then draw a line through the first *and* last in the new order.

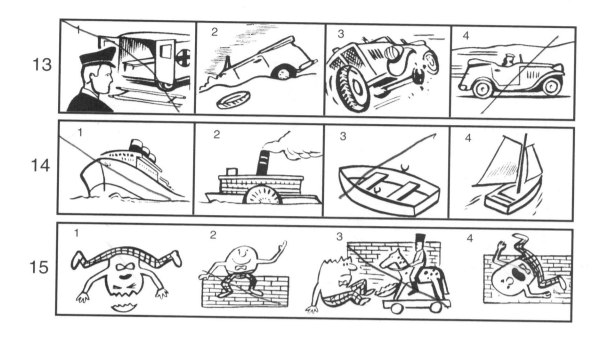

Draw a line through the picture which doesn't belong to the group.

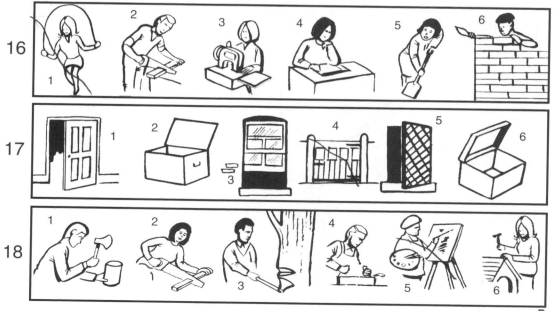

5

Which one has something wrong? Draw a line through it.

Put these in a new order. Draw a line through the first and last.

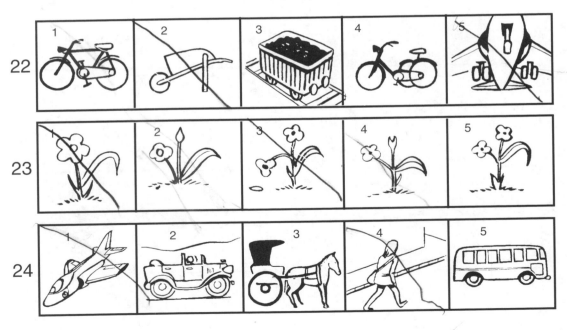

B. Verbal Reasoning: Problems

James has three dogs, called Lex, Ben and Rover. One is white, one is black and one is brown.

The white dog is not called Lex. Lex is not brown. Rover is not brown.

1 So the brown dog is called ....

2 The white dog is called ....

3 The black dog is called ....

Here the words have been mixed up. Find their proper order and then write the answer to each question.

4 a has tails cat many how?   ....

5 the what is coal of colour?   ....

6 fishes legs have do?   ....

7 how eyes many you have?   ....

8 which Christmas month in is?   ....

Helen has one sister, Natalie, and three brothers, David, Jack and Daniel.

9 How many children are there
   in the family?   (1 | 2 | 3 | 4 | 5 | 6)

10 How many brothers has Natalie?   (0 | 1 | 2 | 3 | 4 | 5)

11 How many sisters has Natalie?   (0 | 1 | 2 | 3 | 4 | 5)

12 How many sisters has Daniel?   (0 | 1 | 2 | 3 | 4 | 5)

13 How many brothers has Jack?   (0 | 1 | 2 | 3 | 4 | 5)

---

14 Which of the following words contains the sixth letter of the alphabet?

     (horse | forest | cattle | bicycle | watch | puzzle)

15 Which one has legs, but cannot walk?

     (a window | a dog | a worm | a horse | a chair)

16 If the day after tomorrow is Monday, which day of the week is today? ....

There are three women. One goes to work by car, one on a bicycle and one by bus.

    Julia does not go by car.
    The one who goes by bus is not Rachel.
    Rachel does not go by car.
    Jenny and Rachel are friends.

17 So the woman who goes by car is   ....

18 The woman who goes by bus is   ....

19 The woman who goes on a bicycle is   ....

Class	A	B	C	D	E
Girls	17	18	13	14	16
Boys	15	18	17	17	19
Total	32	36	30	31	35

A school has five classes, called A, B, C, D and E.

Class A has 17 girls and 15 boys and so on.

20 Which class has the largest number of boys?

     (A | B | C | D | E)

21 Which class has the smallest number of girls?

     (A | B | C | D | E)

22 Which class is the largest?   (A | B | C | D | E)

23 Which class has equal numbers of boys and girls?

     (A | B | C | D | E)

---

24 If the day before yesterday was Tuesday, what day will it be tomorrow?
....

25 Emma was born in 1985. She has a sister exactly 3 years older. In which year was her sister born?
....

26 John is two years younger than William. William is eight years old. How old is John?
.... years

In our village there are a doctor, a shopkeeper and a teacher. Their surnames are Scott, Davis and Jones.

Scott knows nothing about medicine.
The doctor is not called Jones.
Jones is not the shopkeeper.

27 So the doctor is called ....

28 The shopkeeper is called ....

29 The teacher is called ....

Four boys stand in a line, one behind another. John is first, Bill second, Henry third and Edward fourth. Edward and John change places and Henry and Bill change places.

30 Who is last in the line now?   (John | Bill | Henry | Edward)

31 Who is second in the line now?
(John | Bill | Henry | Edward)

32 Who comes just in front of Henry now?
(John | Bill | Edward | No one)

---

33 A certain class contains twice as many boys as girls. All the boys have dark hair, but only half of the girls have dark hair. Five girls have fair hair. How many pupils are there in the class?
.... pupils

34 I am going on holiday in 11 weeks' time. If today is April 29th, in which *month* do I go on holiday?
....

A, B, C, D and E are five girls.
A and E are tall; the others are short.
C, D and E swim; the others do not swim.
A and C play tennis but not golf; the others play golf.

35 Which of the tall girls swims? ....

36 Which girl plays tennis and swims? ....

37 Which of the tall girls plays tennis? ....

38 Which of the short girls does not swim? ....

39 Which *two* girls play golf and swim? .... and ....

---

40 Which of the following has both wings and claws?

(cat | lobster | butterfly | parrot | lion | aeroplane)

41 Which of the following has legs and eyes but no teeth?

(horse | dog | snake | bird | rabbit | shark)

42 Which of the following lives on land but has no legs?

(beetle | tortoise | snail | ant | fish | bird)

Day	A	B	C	D	E
Sunrise (a.m.)	3.45	3.43	3.43	3.45	3.50
Sunset (p.m.)	8.14	8.18	8.21	8.21	8.18

The table shows the time at which the sun rose and set on each of five days, lettered A to E.

43 On which day was the earliest sunset? (A | B | C | D | E)

44 On how many of the days did the sun rise before 3.45 a.m.?

(1 | 2 | 3 | 4 | 5)

45 On how many of the days did the sun set before 8.20 p.m.?

(1 | 2 | 3 | 4 | 5)

46 Which was the longest day? (A | B | C | D | E)

47 Which was the shortest day? (A | B | C | D | E)

A, B, C, D, E and F are six cargo boats.
Only A, B and C carry meat.
Only A, D and F carry butter.
Only B, E and F carry fruit.

48 Which boat carries both butter and fruit?

(A | B | C | D | E | F)

49 Which boat carries both meat and fruit?

(A | B | C | D | E | F)

50 Which boat carries both meat and butter?

(A | B | C | D | E | F)

51 Which boat carries neither meat nor fruit?

(A | B | C | D | E | F)

---

52 Straight lines are drawn joining a point inside a square to each of the four corners. Into how many parts is the square divided?

(1 | 2 | 4 | 5 | 8 | 12)

53 Peter is John's father, so John is Peter's

(brother | grandfather | son | uncle | father).

54 Diana is Jim's sister and Jim is Tom's brother, so Diana is Tom's   (cousin | sister | aunt | daughter | mother).

Gary had a white mouse. He exchanged this mouse with Kate for a canary, which Kate had obtained from Sam in return for a rabbit. Sam had obtained this canary from George.

55 Who had the canary first of all?   ....

56 Who now has the canary?   ....

57 Who now has the rabbit?   ....

58 If at the end Kate exchanges with George, what will Kate have then?   ....

Anne is shorter than Isabel but taller than Tom, while Peter is taller than Isabel but shorter than Rebecca.

59 Who is the tallest but one?

(Anne | Rebecca | Isabel | Tom | Peter)

60 Who is the shortest?

(Anne | Rebecca | Isabel | Tom | Peter)

61 Who is the shortest but one?

(Anne | Rebecca | Isabel | Tom | Peter)

Crop	1983	1984	1985	1986	1987	1988
Wheat	97	91	96	92	94	89
Potatoes	96	90	84	94	95	96

The table shows how good the harvests of two crops were in each of six years: the higher the figure, the better the harvest.

62 Which year was the best for wheat?

(1983 | 1984 | 1985 | 1986 | 1987 | 1988)

63 How many years separate the harvesting of the worst two potato crops?

(0 | 1 | 2 | 3 | 4 | 5)

64 When did the wheat harvest appear to be most different from the potato crop?

(1983 | 1984 | 1985 | 1986 | 1987 | 1988)

65 When was the rise in the potato harvest greatest from one year to the next? Mark *both* years.

(1983 | 1984 | 1985 | 1986 | 1987 | 1988)

Score ..../65

C. Verbal Reasoning: Symbols

A B C D E F G H I J K L M N O P Q R S T U V W X Y Z

1 Which letter comes midway between D and L in the alphabet?

....

2 Which letter in this set comes nearest the end of the alphabet?
   E L B T W S N I

....

3 Write these four letters in the order they come in the alphabet:
   S O U R

....

4 Two letters in this set come next to one another in the alphabet.
   Write them *both*: W U N K C T I

.... and ....

Underline the one word in each group which *cannot* be made from the word in capitals.

Example: TON   not | no | **too** | on | to

The word *too* is underlined because it cannot be made from TON: 'T' and 'O' are there, but not a second 'O'.

5 CRAM   car | race | mar | arm | arc
6 CREAM   cram | mare | crane | race | care
7 SPITE   tips | pies | step | spies | pets
8 GLOWS   slow | logs | lows | slog | goals

A stands for 4, B stands for 1, C stands for 3 and D stands for 2. So instead of writing 21, we write DB and instead of 1 + 2 = 3, we put B + D = C. The answer to the sum "A − C" is B because 4 − 3 = 1.

9 Write 312 in letters.   ....

10 Write ACD in figures.   ....

11 Add C and D, then take away A.
   What *letter* is the answer?   ....

12 What letter is twice as big as D?   ....

A B C D E F G H I J K L M N O P Q R S T U V W X Y Z

13 If the letters B, E and F were not in the alphabet, the first four letters would be: ....

14 Which letter in this set comes nearest the end of the alphabet? D U N H R K P ....

15 Write the letter that comes most often in this set of letters: C L X M C P L L C P C ....

16 Two letters in this set come next to one another in the alphabet. Write them *both*:

B H O L G Y V .... and ....

Underline the one word which *cannot* be made from the word in capitals.

17	WEST	stew	stem	sew	wet	set
18	TEAM	mate	meat	tame	ate	meet
19	TRAIN	trim	rant	tarn	rain	tar
20	GREAT	grate	agree	rage	gate	tear
21	SLOW	lows	owl	slew	sow	owls
22	LEAP	peel	pale	pal	peal	ale
23	RIDES	side	reside	dries	sire	side

24 If BZAE stands for 'dolt', then AZE stands for
(lot | lob | toll | doll | old).

25 If DIFP stands for 'brag', then PIFD stands for
(age | rag | garb | grab | bar).

26 If MICD stands for 'rose', then IMD stands for
(roe | oar | ore | sore | era).

27 If WUBL stands for 'seat', then LUB stands for
(ate | east | sat | tea | set).

28 If VFOG stands for 'snap', then GOFV stands for
(pans | naps | span | amps | maps).

A B C D E F G H I J K L M N O P Q R S T U V W X Y Z

29 If there are more than 5 letters between G and N
    write O, if not P.   ....

30 If the letters U, X and Z were not in the alphabet,
    the last four letters would be: ....

31 Count how many different letters there are in
    this set: E H L H E N E H N J.
    Write the *number*.   ....

32 Which letter comes only twice in the set below?

    V X W V L K W X K K L X X W V   ....

**Find the rule for each row and then write the letter or set of
letters that should come *next*.**

Example:	A	C	E	G	....................I....................
33	B	E	H	K	....
34	L	J	H	F	....
35	Y	V	S	P	....
36	BC	CD	DE	EF	....
37	BD	EG	HJ	KM	....

38 If BROG stands for 'lamp', then ORG stands for
                    (pal l lap l amp l alp l map).

39 If BONT stands for 'pear', then NBO stands for
                    (ape l pea l are l rap l ear).

40 If YLWS stands for 'coat', then WYS stands for
                    (cat l act l oat l oak l coo).

41 If UGHE stands for 'glow', then HEG stands for
                    (low l log l owl l goal l go).

42 If HIMC stands for 'play', then CMH stands for
                    (pal l alp l yap l pay l lay).

In each question, find the rule by which the second word in each pair has been made out of the first and then complete the third pair.

Example: bin, in; bone, one; bat, ...**at**......

43 cart, cat; pint, pit; seat, ...

44 nip, pin; saw, was; rat, ...

45 slap, pal; draw, war; fees, ...

46 last, loot; mend, mood; pull, ...

---

47 Which two letters occur least often in the word
DISINTERESTED? .... and ....

48 Write the fourth letter of the third month of the year. ....

49 Which letter occurs in the words SEPTEMBER and APRIL
but not in the word COUNTRY? ....

In a code A stands for 3, B for 8, C for 10, D for 12, E for 20, F for 30 and G for 48. Underline your answer to each of these questions.

50 B years ago Kay was D years old. How old is she now?
(A I B I C I D I E I F I G) years

51 D parcels have arrived, but E were due. How many have still to
arrive? (A I B I C I D I E I F I G) parcels

52 How many hours are there from C a.m. to C p.m.?
(A I B I C I D I E I F I G) hours

53 C hours from now it will be B p.m. What is the time now?
(A I B I C I D I E I F I G) a.m.

Here are four words: PAD SOP SAD POD

Below, the same words are put in a different order in code. The code is the same all through. Find the right word for each code:

54 δ β μ .... 56 μ β π ....

55 δ λ π .... 57 μ λ π ....

In each question, underline one word which _cannot_ be made by rearranging all or some of the letters in the word MECHANISATION.

58	those	chosen	shine	stance	chew
59	machine	change	teams	noise	chant
60	shame	mast	mention	miser	teach
61	moths	anthem	scheme	mascot	nation

A B C D E F G H I J K L M N O P Q R S T U V W X Y Z

Find the rule for each row and then write the letter or set of letters that should come _next_:

62	C	F	I	L	....
63	AZ	CY	EX	GW	....
64	ZA	XC	VE	TG	....
65	ST	PQ	MN	JK	....
66	MN	LO	KP	JQ	....

In a certain code the word GET is written as COL and the word HOLD is written as APIN. Write the _code_ word for each of these:

67 THE ....

68 DOLT ....

69 HEDGE ....

The next three words are written in the same code. Write the meaning of each word:

70 CPL ....

71 AOIN ....

72 IPNCO ....

Here are five words:

LEAN   REAL   EARN   NEAR   LANE

Below, the same words are put in code but in a different order. Find the right word for each code.

73   △ + ○ □   ....

74   △ □ + ○   ....

75   □ + × ○   ....

76   ○ □ + ×   ....

77   × □ + △   ....

78 In a certain code the word DAB is written as BAD and the word PART is written as TRAP. How would the word GNAT be written?   ....

79 In another code the word RING is written as GRIN and the word LEAP is written as PLEA. How would the word HINT be written?   ....

80 In yet another code the word SIFT is written as FITS and the word EAST is written as SATE. How would the word MOPE be written?   ....

Score ..../80

D. Verbal Reasoning: Concepts

Example: Look in the brackets for a word that goes with 'cat' just as 'puppy' goes with 'dog'. The word is 'kitten': underline 'kitten'.

dog – puppy .... cat – (fur | play | kitten | young | milk)

Now do these.

1 grass – green ..... snow – (winter | cold | white | storm | flakes)
2 car – driver .... plane – (pilot | air | fly | hostess | wings)
3 three – third ..... four – (half | eight | one | fourth | second)
4 end – stop ..... beginning – (start | try | time | now | first)

What is the best ending? Underline it.

5 A party always has
(ice-cream | paper hats | jelly | fancy-dress | people).
6 A garden always has
(trees | earth | a lawn | a gate | hedges).
7 A school always has
(pupils | a hall | a headmaster | boys | girls).

Think of the best order to put the things in, then mark the first *and* the last in the new order.

Example: pig | <u>elephant</u> | sparrow | <u>fly</u> | horse

8   7 | 1 | 9 | 5 | 3
9   tiny | big | huge | small
10   third | fourth | sixth | fifth | second
11   March | July | June | May | April

Which one doesn't belong with the others? Underline it.

12   groan | moan | wail | sing | weep

13   scowling | laughing | happy | cheerful | smiling

14   aunt | uncle | grandfather | niece | nephew

15   coat | hair | gloves | trousers | hat

Think of the best order to put things in, then underline the first *and* the last in the new order.

16   codfish | whale | shark | goldfish

17   month | week | day | year | fortnight

18   puddle | pond | ocean | lake

19   CD | EF | AB | DE | BC

In each question, look at the first example of a word-pair; underline the best word to make a similar pair.

20   glove – hand ..... shoe – (leather | sole | horse | toes | foot)

21   pillow – bed ..... cushion – (square | chair | soft | feathers | silk)

22   Rome – Italy ..... Paris –
       (French | France | Berlin | capital | Europe)

23   bite – teeth ..... scratch – (hurt | claws | knife | pin | pain)

Underline the best ending for each sentence.

24   A box always has (straw | sides | contents | a lid | wood).

25   A meal always has (food | soup | bread | meat | sauce).

26   A tree always has
       (leaves | a trunk | fruit | berries | nests | blossom).

27   A river always has
       (trees | rocks | a waterfall | water | a bridge).

Which one doesn't belong? Underline it.

28 elf | fairy | goblin | shepherd | pixie
29 saw | axe | knife | scissors | tongs
30 run | step | write | hop | walk
31 hail | sleet | rain | wind | snow

Underline the best word to make a similar pair.

32 boy – son ..... girl – (sonny | twin | sister | daughter | mother)
33 grass – field ..... water – (lake | tap | drink | cold | swim)
34 water – swim ..... ice – (skate | cream | hot | winter | axe)
35 tiny – small ..... huge – (minute | big | little | mass | more)

Underline the best ending.

36 A teapot always has
    (a kettle | tea | a cosy | water | a spout | a cup).
37 An island always has
    (trees | a boat | cliffs | people | mountains | a shore).
38 An coat always has
    (a coat-hanger | pockets | a velvet collar | armholes | a belt).

Which one doesn't belong? Underline it.

39 quilt | blanket | sheet | eiderdown | tablecloth
40 calf | foal | kitten | lamb | horse
41 dull | murky | dismal | stupid | cloudy
42 lock | fix | return | tie | fasten
43 empty | clear | deserted | bare | quiet

In the brackets there is *one* word which is like the three words in capitals but different from all the others. Underline it.

Example: PLUM, PEAR, ORANGE
    (lettuce | wheat | grass | <u>apple</u> | onion)

44 WIPE, MOP, SCRUB
    (serve | wave | finish | mark | sponge)

45 WHISPER, BABBLE, GURGLE
    (murmur | shriek | clatter | bawl | sniff)

46 PAINT, GILD, ENAMEL
    (draw | cover | write | scrub | varnish)

47 KNAVE, VILLAIN, ROGUE
    (raven | rascal | tramp | savage | beggar)

48 APE, BABOON, GORILLA
    (squirrel | zoo | animal | jungle | monkey)

Make similar pairs of words.

49 me – mine .... he – (him | her | she | his | thine)
50 bed – lie ..... chair – (table | sit | cushion | sleep | lift)
51 go – come .... buy – (goods | send | pay | sell | shop)
52 sparrow – beak ..... pig – (sty | snout | hide | pork | trotter)

Underline the one word which is *different* from the rest.

53 picture | drawing | painting | frame | photograph | portrait
54 tree | bush | earth | grass | vegetable | flower
55 decide | search | investigate | examine | seek
56 trawler | cruiser | submarine | battleship | liner | cargo-boat

---

Think of the best order, then mark the first _and_ last in the new order.

57	youth	|	baby	|	toddler	|	adult	| schoolgirl
58	mansion	|	palace	|	house	|	hut	| cottage
59	city	|	room	|	house	|	village	| town
60	o	|	u	|	e	|	i	| a

Which word is like the three in capitals but different from all the others?

61 NEEDLE, THORN, TACK
      (thread | spike | sew | saw | sharp)

62 HANDCUFFED, MUZZLED, SHACKLED
      (punished | cruel | afraid | bridled | sad)

63 KINGDOM, COUNTRY, DOMINION
      (place | crown | state | royal | capital)

64 MYTH, LEGEND, TALE
      (song | fairy | fable | false | book)

65 CALM, STILL, PEACEFUL
      (closed | disturbed | summer | story | unruffled)

66 AGITATED, DISTURBED, TROUBLED
      (cramped | dizzy | weak | shaken | calm)

Underline the word which means _either_ nearly the same as or nearly the opposite of the word in capitals.

67 ODD (seven | many | number | unusual | four | known)

68 TREMBLE (jump | voice | fear | stamp | shiver | frighten)

69 COLLECT (select | accept | fare | scatter | money | right)

70 SLENDER (quick | receiver | tender | stumble | slime | thick)

71 LEAD (sink | follow | guard | heavy | officer | dog)

Write one letter for each cross.

Example: FINGER is to H......*and*...... as T......*oe*...... is to FOOT.

72 SPEAKER is to S................ as S................ is to SING.

73 CUFF is to S................ as H................ is to ARM.

74 CATTLE is to L................ as S................ is to BLEAT.

75 CLIMBER is to C................ as S................ is to SWIM.

76 NOBODY is to N................ as S................ is to SOMETHING.

The words in each of the groups A to E are alike in some way but different from the words in the other groups.

A	B	C	D	E
wood	store	mill	tool	harbour
coal	pantry	workshop	engine	jetty
cement	depot	pottery	wheel	wharf

Find which is the correct group for each of the words below and write the group letter beside the word.

Example: timber ......**A**...... larder ......**B**......

77 machine ....   82 metal ....

78 quay ....   83 factory ....

79 crafts ....   84 clay ....

80 lever ....   85 barn ....

81 cellar ....

Score ..../85

E. Non-verbal Reasoning

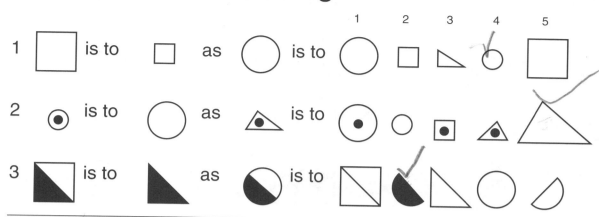

1 ☐ is to ☐ as ◯ is to ...

2 ◉ is to ◯ as △• is to ...

3 ◢ is to ◣ as ◐ is to ...

How many little squares like A make up each shape?

Example:

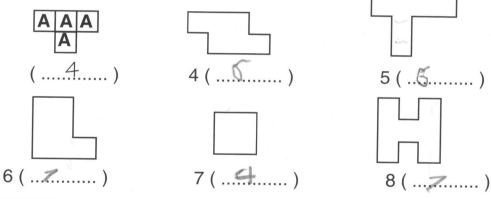

(.....4.....)   4 (.....5.....)   5 (.....6.....)

6 (.....7.....)   7 (.....4.....)   8 (.....7.....)

Which one doesn't belong?

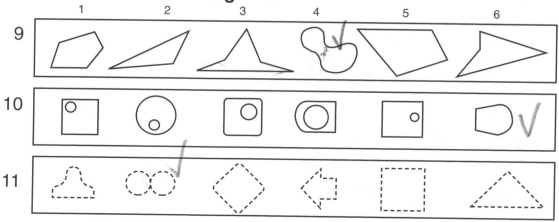

Put these into a new order and mark the first and last.

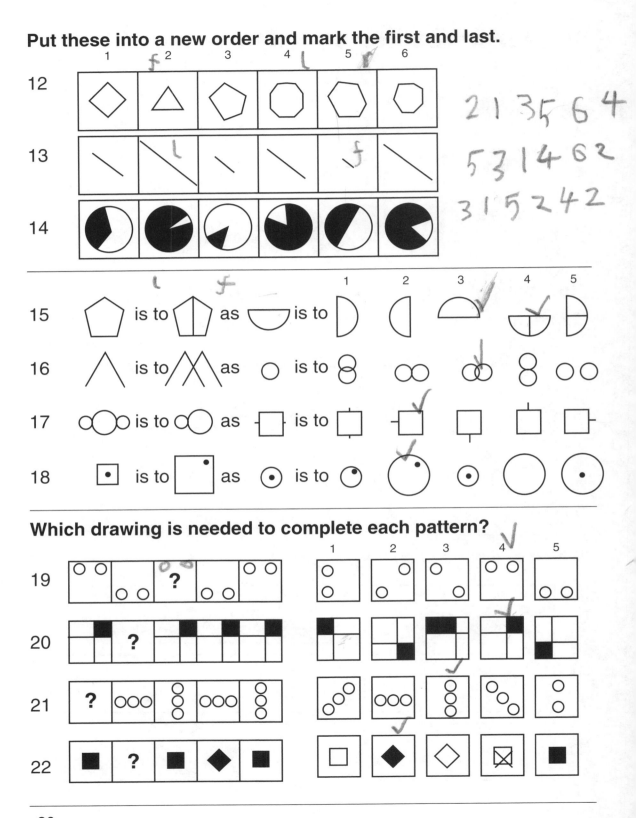

12

13

14

21 35 6 4
5 3 1 4 6 2
3 1 5 2 4 2

15   ⬠ is to ⬠ as ◡ is to

16   △ is to ⋀⋀ as ○ is to

17   ○○○ is to ○○ as ⊣□ is to

18   ▫ is to ☐ as ⊙ is to

Which drawing is needed to complete each pattern?

19

20

21

22

26

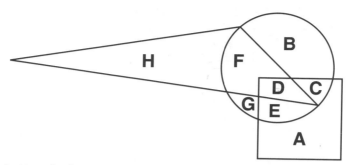

23 Which letter is in the square, but not in the circle or the triangle? ......A.........

24 Which letter is in the circle and the triangle, but not in the square? ......F.....

25 Which letter is in the circle and the triangle and the square? ...D.........

26 Which *two* letters are in the circle, but not in the square or the triangle? ......B........ and ...G........

Put these into a new order and mark the first and last.

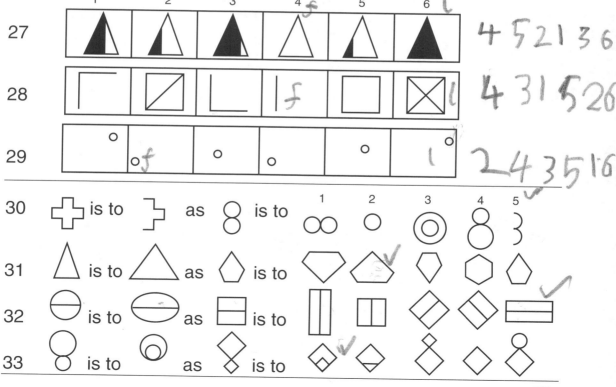

27 4 5 2 1 3 6

28 4 3 1 5 2 6

29 2 4 3 5 1 6

30

31

32

33

Which one looks the same, but is facing the other way?

34

35

36

37

Write the missing number.

38   9, 8, 7, 6, ...

39   1, 4, 7, 10, ...

40   13, 11, 9, 7, ...

41   16, 8, 4, 2, ...

42   23, 29, 35, 41, ...

43   35, 30, ... , 20, 15

44   5, 14, 23, ... , 41

45   0, 1, 3, 6, ...

Put these into a new order and mark the first and last.

46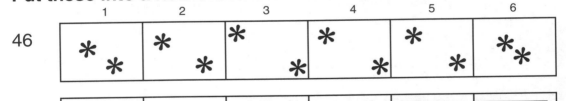

47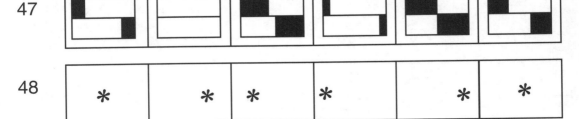

48

28

How many little squares like A make up each shape?

Example:

 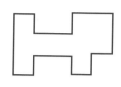 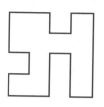 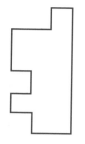 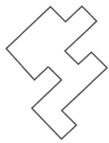

(....4....)   49 (..........) 50 (..........) 51 (.........) 52 (.........)

Which drawing is needed to complete each pattern?

53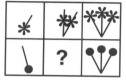

54

55

Write the missing number.

56   64, ... , 16, 8, 4, 2

57   2, 5, 9, 14, 20, ...

58   6, 8½, 11, 13½, ...

59   42, 35, 28, 21, ...

60   ½, ¼, ⅛, 1/16, ...

Which drawing is needed to complete each pattern?

61

62

63

---

64 ▽ is to △ as ⌂ is to

65 is to as is to

66 + −   is to * ○   as ○ □   is to
   ○ *   − +   ■ ●

Which one looks the same, but is facing the other way?

67

68

69

70

Score ..../70

30

Answers

Pages 3–6. **A. Picture Reasoning**

1. 3	2. 6	3. 3	4. 2	5. 2	6. 5
7. 2	8. 3	9. 2	10. 1	11. 5	12. 5
13. 4/1	14. 3/1	15. 2/3	16. 1	17. 4	18. 5
19. 2	20. 5	21. 4	22. 2/5	23. 1/3	24. 4/1

Pages 7–12. **B. Verbal Reasoning: Problems**

1. Ben	2. Rover	3. Lex	4. one	5. black
6. no	7. two	8. December	9. five	10. three
11. one	12. two	13. two	14. forest	15. a chair
16. Saturday	17. Jenny	18. Julia	19. Rachel	20. E
21. C	22. B	23. B	24. Friday	25. 1982
26. six	27. Davis	28. Scott	29. Jones	30. John
31. Henry	32. Edward	33. 30	34. July	35. E
36. C	37. A	38. B	39. D and E	40. parrot
41. bird	42. snail	43. A	44. two	45. three
46. C	47. E	48. F	49. B	50. A
51. D	52. four	53. son	54. sister	55. George
56. Gary	57. Sam	58. nothing	59. Peter	60. Tom
61. Anne	62. 1983	63. one	64. 1985	65. 1985/1986

Pages 13–18. **C. Verbal Reasoning: Symbols**

1. H	2. W	3. ORSU	4. T and U	5. race
6. crane	7. spies	8. goals	9. CBD	10. 432
11. B	12. A	13. ACDG	14. U	15. C
16. G and H	17. stem	18. meet	19. trim	20. agree
21. slew	22. peel	23. reside	24. lot	25. grab
26. ore	27. tea	28. pans	29. O	30. TVWY
31. five	32. L	33. N	34. D	35. M
36. FG	37. NP	38. map	39. ape	40. act
41. owl	42. yap	43. set	44. tar	45. see
46. pool	47. N and R	48. C	49. P	50. E
51. B	52. D	53. C	54. SOP	55. SAD
56. POD	57. PAD	58. chew	59. change	60. miser
61. scheme	62. O	63. IV	64. RI	65. GH
66. IR	67. LAO	68. NPIL	69. AONCO	70. GOT
71. HELD	72. LODGE	73. LANE	74. LEAN	75. EARN
76. NEAR	77. REAL	78. TANG	79. THIN	80. POEM

Pages 19–24. **D. Verbal Reasoning: Concepts**

1. white
2. pilot
3. fourth
4. start
5. people
6. earth
7. pupils
8. 1/9
9. tiny/huge
10. second/sixth
11. March, July
12. sing
13. scowling
14. grandfather
15. hair
16. goldfish/ whale
17. day/year
18. puddle/ocean
19. AB/EF
20. foot
21. chair
22. France
23. claws
24. sides
25. food
26. a trunk
27. water
28. shepherd
29. tongs
30. write
31. wind
32. daughter
33. lake
34. skate
35. big
36. a spout
37. a shore
38. armholes
39. tablecloth
40. horse
41. stupid
42. return
43. quiet
44. sponge
45. murmur
46. varnish
47. rascal
48. monkey
49. his
50. sit
51. sell
52. snout
53. frame
54. earth
55. decide
56. submarine
57. baby/adult
58. hut/palace
59. room/city
60. a/u
61. spike
62. bridled
63. state
64. fable
65. unruffled
66. shaken
67. unusual
68. shiver
69. scatter
70. thick
71. follow
72. SPEAK, SINGER
73. SLEEVE, HAND
74. LOW, SHEEP
75. CLIMB, SWIMMER
76. NOTHING, SOMEBODY
77. D
78. E
79. C
80. D
81. B
82. A
83. C
84. A
85. B

Pages 25–30. **E. Non-verbal Reasoning**

1. four
2. five
3. two
4. six
5. six
6. seven
7. four
8. seven
9. four
10. six
11. two
12. two/four
13. five/two
14. two/three
15. four
16. three
17. two
18. two
19. four
20. four
21. three
22. two
23. A
24. F
25. D
26. B and G
27. four/six
28. four/six
29. two/six
30. five
31. two
32. five
33. one
34. four
35. two
36. five
37. five
38. five
39. 13
40. five
41. one
42. 47
43. 25
44. 32
45. 10
46. six/three
47. two/five
48. four/five
49. 10
50. 12
51. 14
52. 13
53. two
54. five
55. one
56. 32
57. 27
58. 16
59. 14
60. $1/32$
61. two
62. four
63. one
64. one
65. two
66. two
67. three
68. three
69. two
70. one